CONTEN

Preface 2

Appetizers 4

Sides 12

Breakfast 19

PREFACE

I'm so excited to share this book with you. Imagine turning your meals into experiences, where every recipe connects you a bit more with the world around you. I made this cookbook for those who seek to get outside and embrace the joys, and challenges of cooking outdoors.

I'm sure you'll quickly notice that I've left some seasoning and ingredient measurements a bit open-ended. That's because I believe the best flavors come when you trust your gut—literally! Cooking, to me, is a blend of intuition and creativity, not necessarily precision. So go ahead and trust your taste buds to lead you to what feels right.

By the way, most recipes in this book assume that you have your heat source already started and warming up. Just wanted to say that here instead of writing it on almost every page. And because cooking outdoors can bring some challenges, having your tools and fire ready ensures that your cooking experience flows seamlessly. One of my very great friends, Roberto Valenzuela, once taught me the concept of "mise en place." The French culinary principle meaning, "everything in its place." Before you begin, gather and organize all your ingredients and equipment. This practice not only streamlines the cooking process but also allows you to focus on the joy of creating and sharing your meals.

So as you dive into these recipes, think of them as a starting point. Play around with what you've got, mix in some local flavors, and don't be shy about putting your own spin on things. After all, cooking outdoors is all about the adventure!

Finally, while you're out there, I encourage you to take advantage of that time and disconnect from the hustle of your daily life. These recipes are meant to be a backdrop for creating memories, laughing with friends and family, and being able to enjoy the present.

So here's to many delicious meals ahead. As I always say, Enjoy The Journey, and may each dish be as delightful as the company you share it with.

Bon appétit!

APPETIZERS

GRILLED SHRIMP SKEWERS

INGREDIENTS

- 2lbs (~30) Colossal Shrimp (thawed)
- Olive oil
- Lemon juice
- Salt
- Black pepper
- Oregano
- Smoked paprika
- Garlic powder
- Bamboo skewers
- Chopped parsley for serving
- Lemon slices for serving

PREFERRED GRILLING METHODS
- Metal grate over open fire or hot coals
- Charcoal BBQ

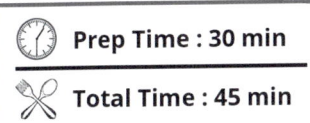

Prep Time : 30 min
Total Time : 45 min

INSTRUCTIONS

- Place the olive oil, lemon juice, salt, pepper, oregano, paprika and garlic powder in a large bowl; whisk to combine.
- Add the shrimp to the bowl and mix gently to coat evenly with the marinade. Marinate for at least 15 minutes or up to 1.5 hours max.
- While the shrimp are in the marinade, soak the skewers in water.
- Skewer 4-6 shrimp on each soaked skewer and place on a plate while skewering the remaining shrimp.
- Cook the shrimp for 2-3 minutes on each side over the hot coals or fire.
- Serve warm with fresh parsley and lemon slices, if desired.

NOTES:

Don't marinate the shrimp longer than 2 hours. The acid from the lemon juice can actually cook the shrimp without any heat. I prefer a 30 minute marinade which is also when the skewers can soak in water. Shrimp cook super fast, and only need 2 to 3 minutes each side. If you overcook them, they lose their juiciness and become rubbery.

CHICKEN QUESADILLAS

INGREDIENTS

- Flour tortillas
- Cooked chicken (chopped or shredded)
- Shredded cheese
- Green or red bell pepper (diced)
- White onion (diced)
- Chopped pre-cooked bacon
- Oil, butter, or tallow for greasing pan

OPTIONAL TOPPINGS

- Salsa
- Guacamole
- Sour cream
- Queso
- Pico de gallo

PREFERRED GRILLING METHODS

- Cast iron skillet or griddle

Prep Time : 5 min
Total Time : 15 min

INSTRUCTIONS

- Preheat pan or griddle over medium-high heat
- Add peppers and onion to an oiled skillet and saute until onions become slightly translucent. Mix in the shredded chicken and bacon until warmed.
- Remove and set aside in a bowl.
- Re-oil skillet or griddle as needed.
- Lay tortillas onto the skillet or griddle and spoon the mixture onto half of the tortilla and cover with cheese.
- Fold the tortilla over and cook until slightly golden brown.
- Flip and cook until slightly golden brown
- Remove from heat and serve immediately.

NOTES:

I love using rotisserie chicken and shredding ahead of time for easier prep. For cheese I always recommend Monterey Jack on quesadillas or a Mexican-style mix. And always feel free to season as you like. This is one of the easiest things to make and a great way for kids to start getting more comfortable and confident to try other dishes.

FLATBREAD MARGHERITA PIZZA

INGREDIENTS

- Premade flatbread or Naan bread
- Marinara sauce
- Fresh mozzarella cheese
- Thinly sliced roma tomatoes
- 6-8 fresh basil leaves
- Minced garlic
- Olive oil

PREFERRED GRILLING METHODS
- Covered cast iron skillet
- Shallow dutch oven

Prep Time : 5 min
Total Time : 20 min

INSTRUCTIONS

- Mix garlic and olive oil together.
- Brush the flatbread with oil & garlic and place in preheated "covered" skillet for 5-8 minutes or until slightly crispy
- Remove from skillet.
- Quickly spread a few tablespoons of marinara on the flatbread and cover with mozzarella, tomato slices and freshly chopped basil.
- Place flatbread back on the covered skillet for another 5 minutes, or until cheese is melted and starting to turn a golden brown.
- Remove from the skillet and top with a bit more freshly chopped basil if desired.
- Slice and serve hot, and enjoy!

NOTES:

Flatbread is easy to make ahead of time and bring with you in a ziploc. For easier planning, you can also grab a few bags of Naan bread. Normally, I like to use slices of thick, low-moisture mozzarella on my Margherita pizza. But when I'm camping, I tend to usually bring shredded cheese as I use that with other recipes. Feel free to make it how you like.

GRILLED STUFFED MUSHROOMS

INGREDIENTS

- 8-10 baby portobello mushrooms
- 8 ounces cream cheese
- Shredded cheese (your choice)
- 1/2 lb ground Italian sausage
- Salt and pepper to taste
- Garlic powder to taste
- Italian breadcrumbs
- Chopped parsley

PREFERRED GRILLING METHODS
- Metal grate over indirect heat
- Charcoal BBQ

 Prep Time : 10 min

 Total Time : 30 min

INSTRUCTIONS

- Remove the stems and using a damp paper towel, thoroughly clean each mushroom
- Combine cream cheese, cheddar cheese, cooked ground Italian sausage, salt and black pepper, and garlic powder in a bowl and mix until well combined.
- Stuff each mushroom with the combined mixture making sure to not overfill.
- Sprinkle the tops with Italian breadcrumbs and chopped parsley.
- Place the stuffed mushrooms over indirect heat and grill for 15-20 minutes or until the cheese is melted and the filling is warmed through. I also like to cover the mushrooms for the last 5-10 minutes to cooked faster.

NOTES:

If you don't want to waste the stems, you can finely dice them and combine them into the filling. Depending on how you are cooking these, you might have to get creative. I've put them onto foil to prevent them from burning and also covered with a lid to help melt the cheese.

BUFFALO CAULIFLOWER BITES

INGREDIENTS

- 1 head cauliflower, cut into pieces
- 5 tbsps olive oil
- 1/2 cup Franks red hot sauce
- ½ cup butter
- Garlic powder
- Worcestershire sauce

PREFERRED GRILLING METHODS
- Metal grate over fire and coals
- Charcoal BBQ

 Prep Time : 5 min

 Total Time : 20 min

INSTRUCTIONS

- Melt butter and mix in garlic powder. Once combined, add hot sauce and one dash of Worcestershire sauce. Let sauce simmer on low heat to combine ingredients.
- Toss cauliflower in olive oil to give very light coating.
- Grill cauliflower florets until they have a nice char on the outside, but not burnt, and all sides have touched the grill. This should take about 15 minutes.
- Remove from heat and toss cauliflower in the sauce.
- Serve immediately and enjoy!

NOTES:

Grilling the cauliflower directly on the grates adds flavor and char and takes this vegetable to a completely different level.

PROSCIUTTO WRAPPED ASPARAGUS

INGREDIENTS

- Thinly sliced prosciutto
- Medium asparagus spears
- Olive oil
- Ground black pepper
- Grated parmesan (optional)

PREFERRED GRILLING METHODS
- Metal grate over indirect heat
- Charcoal BBQ

 Prep Time : 5 min

 Total Time : 20 min

INSTRUCTIONS

- Trim the ends off of the asparagus spears
- Soak asparagus in cold water while you prep your grill or get your fire started. This will allow the asparagus to absorb a little moisture and stay crisp and moist while grilling.
- Drain asparagus and brush with a little olive oil. Not too much just a little, Season to taste with black pepper and garlic powder.
- Lay slices of prosciutto down and roll up asparagus spears tightly.
- Cook asparagus until tender and prosciutto crisps, about 4-5 minutes per side.
- Remove from grill and drizzle with a little extra olive oil and fresh black pepper.

NOTES:

> Use asparagus spears that are not too small but not too large. This will allow them to cook evenly without burning or being undercooked. Another great touch before serving is to top with freshly grated parmesan.

STUFFED JALAPEÑOS

INGREDIENTS

- 7 whole jalapeños
- 14 strips bacon
- 8 ounces cream cheese (room temp)
- Salt and pepper to taste
- Smoked paprika
- Garlic powder
- Cheddar cheese

PREFERRED GRILLING METHODS
- Metal grate over indirect heat
- Charcoal BBQ

 Prep Time : 5 min
 Total Time : 35 min

INSTRUCTIONS

- Wash the jalapeños. Remove the stem and cut them into halves. Deseed the core and take away the membrane.
- Combine softened cream cheese, cheddar cheese, salt, pepper, smoked paprika, and garlic powder into a bowl. Mix the ingredients until well combined.
- Fill the jalapeño halves with the cream cheese mixture.
- Wrap the bacon strips around the filled jalapeño halves. You may need to insert a toothpick to hold the bacon in place.
- Grill the jalapeños on indirect heat for 25 minutes or until bacon is done.

NOTES:

If you plan on making these when you're outdoors. I like to pre-slice and deseed the jalapeños ahead of time so they are ready to go when you decide to make them.

SIDES

SMOKED BACON MAC & CHEESE

INGREDIENTS

- 1 box elbow macaroni noodles
- 1/2 cup butter
- 5 tablespoons smoked flour
- Smoked paprika
- Fresh black pepper to taste
- Garlic parmesan seasoning
- 2 cups half and half
- 1 lb cooked bacon (chopped)
- 1 ½ cups cheddar cheese
- 1 ½ cups Monterey jack cheese
- 1 ½ cups gouda cheese

PREFERRED COOKING METHOD
- Cast iron skillet

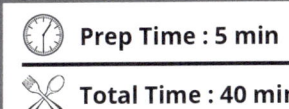

Prep Time : 5 min
Total Time : 40 min

INSTRUCTIONS

- Boil noodles in a large pot of salted water until al dente. Strain and set aside.
- In a cast iron skillet, melt butter and then whisk in the flour until a smooth paste forms.
- Carefully whisk in the half and half along with all of your seasonings and bring the sauce up to a boil. Remove from direct heat.
- Slowly mix in all of the cheeses and stir until melted.
- Add the noodles and half of the chopped bacon and mix gently until fully coated.
- Sprinkle the rest of the chopped bacon over the top of the mac and cheese.
- Place the skillet back over indirect heat, cover with a hot lid, and cook for an additional 5-10 minutes.
- Remove from heat and serve while hot and the cheese is nice and melty!

NOTES:

The secret to this smoked mac and cheese is the flour. One of my favorite things to always have on hand is smoked flour. To do so, spread flour onto baking sheets and smoke on your smoker of choice for a few hours. Then store in Tupperware until needed. Once you've tasted a meal with smoked flour, you'll want to use it with so many other dishes!

WATERMELON FETA SALAD

INGREDIENTS

- 1 small (3lb) watermelon, rind removed, cut into 1-inch chunks
- 1/4 cup extra virgin olive oil
- 2 tablespoons freshly squeezed lime juice or lemon juice (your preference)
- 1/2 teaspoon kosher salt
- Small pinch of freshly ground pepper
- 1/4 cup chopped mint leaves
- 8 ounces crumbled or chopped feta cheese

Prep Time : 5 min
Total Time : 10 min

INSTRUCTIONS

- In a small bowl, whisk together olive oil, citrus juice, salt and pepper.
- Pour the dressing over the chilled diced watermelon along with the mint.
- Toss gently to combine.
- Sprinkle the feta cheese on top and serve immediately.
- *THIS SALAD IS BEST PREPARED JUST BEFORE SERVING

NOTES:

Other great additions you can add to this salad are fresh arugula, basil, cucumber, and even kalamata olives!

GRILLED STREET ELOTES

INGREDIENTS

- 7 ears yellow corn, shucked
- 1/2 cup mayonnaise
- 1/3 cup Mexican crema
- Zest from one lime
- Juice from one lime
- Minced garlic
- Chili powder
- Cayenne pepper
- 1 cup finely crumbled cotija cheese
- Salt and black pepper to taste
- Finely chopped fresh cilantro
- Mexican hot sauce (Tapatio or Cholua)

PREFERRED GRILLING METHODS
- Metal grate over fire and hot coals
- Charcoal BBQ

 Prep Time : 10 min

 Total Time : 20 min

INSTRUCTIONS

- Whisk together mayonnaise, mexican crema, lime zest, lime juice, garlic, chili powder, and cayenne pepper. Lightly season with salt and pepper to taste. Set aside.
- Place corn on metal grate or grill, leaving space between them.
- Grill until charred on all sides, turning every 3 minutes, about 9 minutes total.
- Working with one cob of corn at a time, using a basting brush, brush all sides generously with the seasoned mayonnaise mixture then sprinkle with cotija and chili powder. Finish with cilantro and/or Mexican hot sauce.
- Transfer to a serving platter, serve and enjoy!

NOTES:

If you tend to lean towards the non-spicy side, feel free to leave out or reduce the chili powder and/or cayenne pepper. You can also substitute the crema with sour cream.

STUFFED ROMAINE HEARTS

INGREDIENTS

- 3 romaine hearts
- Grape tomatoes
- 1 sweet or vidalia onion
- Cooked chopped bacon
- Balsamic vinegar
- Olive oil
- Parmesan cheese
- Freshly ground black pepper

PREFERRED GRILLING METHODS
- Metal grate over fire and hot coals
- Charcoal BBQ

Prep Time : 5 min
Total Time : 25 min

INSTRUCTIONS

- Start by sauteing halved grape tomatoes and sliced onions in olive oil.
- Then add the chopped bacon and two dashes of balsamic vinegar. Once combined and heated, remove from heat and set aside.
- Halve the romaine hearts lengthwise and remove some of the inner core.
- Brush the cut surfaces of the lettuce with olive oil.
- Grill the hearts, cut side down, for 2 to 2 1/2 minutes on each side, until char marks appear on the surface of the lettuce and it wilts slightly.
- Remove from grill and spoon in the bacon and veggie mixture.
- Top with freshly grated parmesan cheese and black pepper.
- Serve and enjoy!

NOTES:

This is one of those recipes where you can experiment with other sauteed veggies or even other proteins like chicken, steak or shrimp. The possibilities are endless.

CHICKEN QUINOA SALAD

INGREDIENTS

- Cooked quinoa
- Cooked chicken breast
- Ripe avocado
- Red bell pepper
- Grape tomatoes
- Chopped cilantro
- Sweet yellow corn
- Black beans
- Lime juice

INSTRUCTIONS

- Slice or chop avocado, bell pepper, and grape tomatoes.
- Mix together veggies, corn, beans, and sliced chicken.
- Add quinoa to serving bowls and top with the mixed ingredients.
- Enjoy plain or with your favorite dressing.

Prep Time : 5 min
Total Time : 10 min

OPTIONAL DRESSINGS

GREEK DRESSING

- ¼ cup extra-virgin olive oil
- 3 tablespoons red wine vinegar
- 1 tbsp minced garlic
- ½ teaspoon dried oregano
- ¼ teaspoon dijon mustard
- ¼ teaspoon sea salt
- Freshly ground black pepper

** Combine and whisk together

CILANTRO LIME DRESSING

- 2 cups fresh cilantro
- 1 tbsp minced garlic
- ¼ cup fresh lime juice
- 2 teaspoons honey
- ½ teaspoon ground coriander
- ½ teaspoon sea salt
- ½ cup extra-virgin olive oil
- ½ cup whole milk greek yogurt

** Combine and blend until smooth

NOTES:

Feel free to enjoy plain or add your favorite dressing. I included two of my favorites for this. A creamy cilantro lime dressing and a traditional Greek dressing. Both can easily be made ahead of time or something similar bought by the bottle in the store.

FRENCH BREAD PIZZA

INGREDIENTS

- 1 loaf French bread, halved horizontally
- 3 tbsp minced garlic
- Olive oil
- 2 tbsp butter (softened)
- Marinara sauce
- Sliced black olives
- Pepperoni
- Shredded mozzarella
- Grated parmesan
- Dried basil

PREFERRED GRILLING METHODS
- Metal grate over hot coals
- Charcoal BBQ

 Prep Time : 5 min
 Total Time : 15 min

INSTRUCTIONS

- Slice a loaf of French bread horizontally.
- Mix softened butter, minced garlic, and olive oil in a small dish. Spread the mixture on the cut side of the bread.
- Grill (cut side down) for a few minutes to lightly brown and crisp.
- Remove from heat and lightly cover with sauce, cheese, and favorite toppings.
- Put back on grilling surface cut side up. Cover and grill about 5-10 minutes or until cheese is melted and starting to brown.

NOTES:

This has always been a kid favorite and comes together so quickly. For a bigger group I like to grill and have the toasted halves ready to go with ingredients laid out and let everybody make their own.

BREAKFAST

WATERSHED BREAKFAST BURRITOS

INGREDIENTS

- Extra large flour tortillas
- Eggs
- Bacon
- Diced hashbrowns
- Shredded cheese
- Green or red bell pepper (diced)
- White onion (diced)
- Seasonings to taste

PREFERRED GRILLING METHOD
- Cast iron skillet to prepare fillings
- Grate or griddle over coals to finish

Prep Time : 10 min
Total Time : 45 min

INSTRUCTIONS

- In a cast iron skillet, cook bacon until crispy. Transfer bacon to a large bowl. Make sure to leave bacon grease in the skillet.
- Cook the diced hashbrowns in the bacon grease until done. Transfer hashbrowns in the large bowl.
- Add diced bell peppers and onions to the skillet and saute until almost done.
- Add beaten eggs to the skillet. Mix and cook with the peppers and onions.
- When done, remove skillet from heat and mix in shredded cheese and seasonings until incorporated fully. Add to large bowl and mix well.
- Spoon the mixed fillings into tortillas and roll into large burritos.
- Place burritos onto grilling surface to slightly brown.
- Serve and enjoy!

NOTES:

You can also make these burritos ahead of time and wrap in aluminum foil. Then come breakfast time just pop onto hot coals or griddle and rotate every few minutes until the inside is hot and ready to eat. Another time saver for these (and also easier when packing outdoors) is to crack all your eggs into a pourable Tupperware container and shake until beaten well. Then when you're ready to cook, just pour how ever much you need into the skillet.

SMOKED BISCUITS & GRAVY

INGREDIENTS

- Premade biscuit dough or canned
- 1/4 cup smoked all-purpose flour
- 1 lb ground pork breakfast sausage
- 2 to 2.5 cups whole milk
- Salt and Pepper to taste

PREFERRED GRILLING METHODS
- Cast iron skillet with lid
- Dutch oven

Prep Time : 5 min
Total Time : 15 min

INSTRUCTIONS

- Place biscuit dough or premade canned biscuits into a cast iron skillet or dutch oven. Cover and cook until golden brown. Remove from the skillet and set aside while you make the gravy.
- Add the sausage to the skillet. Smash and mix until it's crumbled. Continue to cook stirring occasionally until it starts to brown. Do not drain the grease away.
- Sprinkle the flour over the sausage and stir. Cook for 2 to 3 minutes, stirring constantly.
- Gradually add the milk, stirring well after each addition. Reduce to a simmer and allow the gravy to thicken, stirring frequently. For thicker gravy, add about 2 cups total. For thinner gravy, add more milk. Add salt and lots of black pepper to taste. Serve over the top of the biscuits and enjoy!

NOTES:

> This is the recipe that inspired me to experiment with smoking my all purpose flour! I wanted a smoky flavor to my gravy so when I first used the smoked flour with this and tasted it, I knew I hit the jackpot.

STUFFED FRENCH TOAST

INGREDIENTS

- Thick bread slices
- 3 eggs
- 1/3 cup milk
- Cinnamon
- Peanut butter
- Strawberry jelly
- Powdered sugar

PREFERRED GRILLING METHOD
- Cast iron skillet or griddle

Prep Time : 5 min
Total Time : 15 min

INSTRUCTIONS

- Mix eggs, milk, and cinnamon in a flat dish.
- Spread peanut butter on one slice of bread.
- Spread jelly on another slice of bread.
- Put the pieces together and lay each both sides into the egg mixture.
- Place directly onto the hot skillet or griddle and cook for 2-3 minutes each side.
- Repeat with the rest of the bread and egg mixture.
- Slice and sprinkle with powdered sugar and serve.

NOTES:

This idea came about when I did a video series called "TWLPT" (Thing We Love Put Together) And this was by far a favorite for both me and my kids. I also love adding some sliced strawberries on the side.

BACON PANCAKES

INGREDIENTS

- 1⅓ cups all-purpose flour
- 1 tablespoon baking powder
- 2 tablespoons granulated sugar
- 1 teaspoon salt
- 1.5 cup milk
- 1 large egg
- 4 tablespoons butter melted
- 1 tablespoon vanilla extract
- Cooked bacon
- Maple syrup

PREFERRED COOKING METHOD
- Cast iron skillet or griddle

Prep Time : 5 min
Total Time : 20 min

INSTRUCTIONS

- Cook the bacon to your liking and set the bacon grease aside to use with the pancakes.
- Whisk the flour, sugar, baking powder, and salt in a large bowl.
- In a medium bowl whisk together the milk, egg, melted butter, and vanilla.
- Pour the milk mixture into the flour and fold together until well combined.
- Lightly grease the cooking surface by brushing with the leftover bacon grease.
- Lay full strips of bacon down and carefully cover it with the pancake batter.
- Cook for a few minutes until golden on the bottom and bubbles start to appear on the top, then flip over and cook an additional minute or until golden brown.
- Add more bacon grease with each new batch of bacon and pancakes.
- Serve hot and dip into maple syrup to enjoy!

NOTES:

You can speed this recipe up by using premade pancake mix and pre-cooked bacon. But if you do decide to make this pancake recipe you'll have a hard time going back to the premade mix.

SAUSAGE & POTATO HASH

INGREDIENTS

- 1.5 lbs diced potatoes
- 1lb ground Italian mild sausage
- 8 large eggs
- 1 small white onion (diced)
- Red and green bell pepper (chopped)
- Salt and pepper to taste
- Olive oil
- Minced garlic
- Red pepper flakes

PREFERRED COOKING METHOD
- Cast iron skillet

Prep Time : 10 min
Total Time : 40 min

INSTRUCTIONS

- Add olive oil and diced potatoes in a large skillet. Season with salt and pepper, and cook for 7-10 minutes, until about halfway cooked through, stirring occasionally.
- Add the diced onion and cook for another 3 minutes, stirring occasionally.
- Add the sausage, bell peppers, garlic and red pepper flakes to the skillet and stir.
- Continue cooking until potatoes are cooked through, about another 10 minutes.
- You can also cover the skillet, this will cook the potatoes a bit faster.
- Once potatoes are done, make a spot in the middle to pour the beaten eggs.
- Scramble the eggs and slowly incorporate the rest of the skillet all together.
- Taste for seasoning and adjust with salt and pepper if needed.
- Serve hot and enjoy!

NOTES:

This has always been a go-to breakfast when the kids are starving or we have a big day ahead of us. And if you have a larger group, you can easily adjust the amount of hashbrowns and eggs to make sure everybody gets their fill.

EARLY BIRD DONUT HOLES

INGREDIENTS

- 1/2 cup White Sugar
- 3 Tablespoons Cinnamon
- 1 can Pre-made Biscuit Dough
- Oil for frying

PREFERRED COOKING METHOD
- Cast iron pot or dutch oven

Prep Time : 5 min
Total Time : 15 min

INSTRUCTIONS

- Combine sugar and cinnamon in a small bowl. Set aside.
- Line a plate with paper towels and set aside.
- Place your frying oil in a Dutch oven or cast iron pot over your heat source. Use a candy thermometer to ensure you bring the oil to 350F.
- Cut each biscuit into thirds or fourths
- Shape the dough by rolling it in your hands into similarly sized balls.
- Once oil is hot, fry donut holes in batches for 1 minute or until golden brown.
- Set fried donut holes on the paper towel-lined plate for a minute to cool.
- While still warm, transfer to the bowl with cinnamon and sugar and swirl to coat.
- Remove to a serving plate
- Repeat until all donut holes have been fried and coated.
- Serve and enjoy!

NOTES:

This recipe couldn't be any easier to make. The only negative to making this for the kids though, is once you make it once, they will want it everyday!

SUNRISE CASSEROLE

INGREDIENTS

- 1 lb ground pork breakfast sausage
- 1 green bell pepper (diced)
- 1 red bell pepper (diced)
- 1 small white onion (diced)
- 3 cups frozen hash brown potatoes
- Shredded cheddar cheese
- 1 cup Bisquick mix
- 2 cups milk
- 6 large eggs
- Salt and pepper to taste.

PREFERRED GRILLING METHOD
- Dutch oven or skillet with lid

Prep Time : 15 min
Total Time : 60 min

INSTRUCTIONS

- In dutch oven or skillet, cook sausage, bell pepper and onion about 10 to 12 minutes, stirring occasionally, until sausage is no longer pink.
- Add and mix in potatoes and 1 1/2 cups of cheese to the sausage mixture.
- In a medium bowl, whisk Bisquick, eggs and milk together.
- Pour and mix into skillet with other ingredients.
- Cover and cook 30 to 40 minutes or until knife inserted in center comes out clean. Top with more cheese. Bake 2 minutes longer or until cheese is melted.
- Let stand 5 minutes before serving.
- Serve and enjoy!

NOTES:

You can really elevate this recipe by replacing the cheddar with smoked Gouda cheese and apple sausage. Get creative and see what other combinations you can come up with.

CHELAN STYLE CALZONES

INGREDIENTS

- 2 cans crescent dough sheets
- 8 large eggs
- 2 tbsp butter
- 1/2 lb smoked honey ham (diced)
- 1/2 red bell pepper (diced)
- 1/2 green bell pepper (diced)
- Shredded cheddar cheese
- Shredded swiss cheese
- 1/4 cup green onions (diced)

PREFERRED COOKING METHOD
- Dutch oven

Prep Time : 10 min

Total Time : 35 min

INSTRUCTIONS

- Add 1 tbsp butter and eggs to dutch oven and scramble. Remove and set aside.
- Add diced bell peppers and 1 tbsp butter to dutch oven and cook for 3-4 minutes. Remove and add to scrambled eggs.
- Mix diced ham, green onions, cheddar and swiss cheese with eggs and peppers.
- Roll out crescent dough sheets and cut to desired size.
- Spoon the egg, ham, and cheese mixture on half of crescent dough.
- Fold the other half over and pinch together sides.
- Spray dutch oven with cooking spray to prevent dough from sticking.
- Cover and cook for 10-15 minutes or until golden brown.
- Remove and let sit for a few minutes before serving. Enjoy!

NOTES:

I love using rotisserie chicken and shredding ahead of time for easier prep. For cheese I always recommend Monterey Jack on quesadillas or a Mexican-style mix. And always feel free to season as you like.

FIRE CRUSTED QUICHE

INGREDIENTS

- 1 pie crust
- 8 eggs
- 1 cup heavy cream
- Shredded sharp cheddar cheese
- 1 lb pork ground sausage
- 1/2 red bell pepper (diced)
- 1/2 green bell pepper (diced)
- 1/2 white onion (diced)
- Salt and pepper to taste

PREFERRED GRILLING METHOD
- Cast iron skillet

Prep Time : 10 min
Total Time : 60 min

INSTRUCTIONS

- Add your sausage to the skillet, stir frequently and cook until browned.
- While your sausage cooks, whisk your eggs, cream, salt and pepper.
- Remove sausage from skillet and some of the grease.
- Roll out your pie crust and place in the bottom of the skillet.
- To build your quiche, place the cooked sausage in the bottom, top with cheese, peppers and onions and add your egg mixture on top.
- Cover and cook for 35 -45 minutes or until your eggs are set.
- Cut, serve, and enjoy!

NOTES:

You know how sometimes you order a pizza with half pepperoni and half olives. Well now that my kids finally started enjoying a good quiche, they started coming up with their own combinations. Now we usually make this where each of my boys build one half of it with their favorite ingredients to make it their own.

HONEY BUTTER CORNBREAD

INGREDIENTS

- 1 ½ cups fine yellow cornmeal
- ½ cup all-purpose flour
- ¼ cup packed dark brown sugar
- 2 teaspoons kosher salt
- 1 tablespoon baking powder
- ½ teaspoon baking soda
- 1 ½ cups buttermilk
- 3 tablespoons honey
- 2 large eggs
- ½ cup (1 stick) unsalted butter (melted)
- 2 tbsp unsalted butter, for skillet

HONEY BUTTER TOPPING

- 3 tbps salted or unsalted melted butter
- 4 tbsp honey

PREFERRED GRILLING METHOD
- Cast iron skillet

Prep Time : 10 min
Total Time : 35 min

INSTRUCTIONS

- In a large bowl, whisk together the cornmeal, flour, brown sugar, salt, baking powder, and baking soda, then set the bowl aside.
- In another medium bowl, whisk together the buttermilk, honey, and eggs.
- Pour the wet ingredients into the cornmeal/flour mixture and use a rubber spatula to mix until just combined. Be careful not to over-mix.
- Pour in the ½ cup melted butter and use the same rubber spatula to fold the melted butter into the batter, again, until just combined without over-mixing.
- Melt 2 tbsp of butter into a preheated skillet and use a pastry brush to grease the bottom and sides of the skillet.
- Pour the batter into the heated skillet. Use a spatula to smooth the top as needed.
- Cover and cook the cornbread until set, about 20-25 minutes or until a toothpick inserted into the center of the cornbread comes out clean.
- For the honey butter topping, in a small bowl, whisk together the melted butter and honey until combined. Immediately pour it over the hot cornbread and spread to cover the surface. Let it sit for 2-3 minutes to soak in nicely.
- Slice into squares or wedges and serve warm. Enjoy!

ENTREES

BEEF STEW

INGREDIENTS

- 3 lb beef chuck roast, well trimmed and cut into 2" pieces
- Salt and pepper to taste
- 2 medium onions, cut into 1" thick slices
- Olive oil
- 4 tbsp minced garlic
- 1 lb medium carrots, cut into 1-inch pieces
- 4 tbsp all-purpose flour
- 1 can Guinness Extra Stout or other stout
- 3 cups chicken stock
- 1 6-oz can tomato paste
- 1 lb. Yukon gold potatoes, cut into 1-inch pieces
- 8 sprigs thyme, tied together
- 2 bay leaves
- 1/2 cup fresh parsley (chopped)

PREFERRED COOKING METHOD
- Dutch oven

Prep Time : 30 min
Total Time : 3 hours

INSTRUCTIONS

- Heat oil in a dutch oven. Add beef and season with salt and pepper. Cook and turn occasionally to make sure all sides are browned, 4 to 5 minutes, adding more oil if needed. Transfer beef to a bowl.
- Remove from direct heat. Add onion to dutch oven and cook, stirring occasionally, until soft, 4 to 6 minutes.
- Add garlic and carrots, stirring occasionally until almost soft, 3 to 5 minutes.
- Sprinkle flour over vegetables and stir for about 2 minutes.
- Add Guinness and cook, scraping up any browned bits, until starting to thicken
- Add stock and tomato paste and stir to combine.
- Add beef, potatoes, thyme, and bay leaves.
- Cover and simmer, stirring occasionally, 1 1/2 hours.
- Remove lid and cook, uncovered, until beef is very tender, 45 to 60 minutes
- Discard thyme and bay leaves. Season with salt and pepper.
- Garnish with parsley, serve and enjoy!

BACK COUNTRY LASAGNA

INGREDIENTS

- 1 lb ground sweet Italian sausage
- 1 lb ground beef
- 2 tbsp minced garlic
- 1/2 white onion (chopped)
- 1 cup chicken stock
- 2 cups marinara sauce
- 1 tbsp dried oregano
- 1 box (8-10 ounce) lasagna noodles
- 1 cup fresh basil, roughly chopped
- 1 cup ricotta cheese
- 2 cups shredded mozzarella
- 4 tbsp grated parmesan
- Olive oil

PREFERRED COOKING METHOD
- Dutch oven

Prep Time : 5 min
Total Time : 40 min

INSTRUCTIONS

- Heat oil in a dutch oven.
- Add sausage and beef, breaking it up and stirring until beginning to brown.
- Add chopped onion and stir until it starts to look translucent.
- Add garlic and cook, stirring, until fragrant.
- Add chicken stock, marinara, and oregano.
- Nestle pasta pieces in the mixture, and bring to a boil.
- Remove from direct heat and simmer uncovered, stirring occasionally, until pasta is tender. About 10-12 min.
- Mix in the basil and ricotta and then top with mozzarella and Parmesan.
- Cover and cook for about 5 minutes or until cheese is melted and golden.
- Remove from heat and let cool before serving.

NOTES:

You can also make this more traditionally by boiling the lasagna separately and layering everything together. But I tend to like this version when I'm outdoors.

CHICKEN AND POTATO CHOWDER

INGREDIENTS

- 1lb hickory bacon (chopped)
- 1 tbsp unsalted butter
- 2 tbsp minced garlic
- 1 leek (halved and sliced)
- 1 tsp ground fennel seed
- 3 tbsp all-purpose flour
- 2 cups whole milk
- 4 cups chicken stock
- 1lb red potatoes cut into 1/2" chunks
- 5 sprigs thyme
- Salt and pepper to taste
- 2 cups shredded rotisserie chicken
- 1 cup frozen corn (thawed)
- Sliced fresh chives, for serving

PREFERRED COOKING METHOD
- Dutch oven

Prep Time : 5 min
Total Time : 15 min

INSTRUCTIONS

- Cook bacon in dutch oven until browned and crisp, then remove and set aside.
- Add butter and leek to dutch oven.
- Cook and stir occasionally until just tender, around 3 to 4 minutes.
- Add garlic and fennel. Cook while stirring until fragrant.
- Add flour and stir for about a minute, then slowly whisk in milk and then stock.
- Add potatoes and thyme. Season with salt and pepper.
- Bring to a boil then remove from direct heat. Simmer until potatoes are fork tender, about 14 to 16 minutes.
- Add chicken and corn. Cook until soup is heated through, about 2-3 minutes.
- Discard thyme and serve topped with fresh chives.

NOTES:

> For some reason the ocean always makes me crave some type of chowder. My kids aren't huge clam chowder fans, but this one they love.

DUTCH OVEN ENCHILADAS

INGREDIENTS

- Corn tortillas
- Rotisserie chicken (shredded)
- Shredded cheddar cheese
- 1 (10 oz) can green enchilada sauce
- 1 (10 oz) can red enchilada sauce
- 1/2 medium onion (diced)
- 1 (4 oz) can fire roasted diced green chilis
- Cilantro (chopped)
- Sour cream optional for serving.
- Olive oil

INSTRUCTIONS

Prep Time : 10 min
Total Time : 60 min

- In a medium bowl, mix the chicken, red enchilada sauce, onion, some cilantro and lots of shredded cheese.
- Evenly split the chicken mixture on the tortillas and roll them up.
- Spray the bottom and sides of your Dutch oven with cooking spray.
- Pour 1/4 of the green enchilada sauce in the bottom of the Dutch oven.
- Lay the rolled tortillas in the sauce in the dutch oven with the seam side down.
- Pour the remaining green enchilada sauce over the top of the enchiladas.
- Cover the dutch oven with its lid (and coals) and bake for 35-40 minutes until the enchiladas are heated through. Turn the dutch oven and lid 1/4 turn in opposite directions every 10-15 minutes for even baking.
- Remove the cover and sprinkle more cheese over the enchiladas.
- Put lid back on (with coals) and continue baking (about 5 minutes) until the cheese melts.
- Remove from heat and let stand for about 10 minutes to firm the enchiladas.
- Serve topped with sour cream and cilantro, if desired. Enjoy!

NOTES:

To save yourself some time and clean up, you can make your enchilada filling at home ahead of time. Store it in a container in your cooler until ready to use. At camp, just skip ahead to the enchilada rolling step, cover with sauce and cheese, and bake in your dutch oven!

STEAK FAJITAS

INGREDIENTS

- Fajita-size flour tortillas
- 1 1/2 pounds flat iron steak
- 1 yellow bell pepper, cut into strips
- 1 red bell pepper, cut into strips
- 1 sweet onion, cut into slices
- Chili powder
- Ground cumin
- Smoked paprika
- Minced garlic
- Salt and pepper to taste
- Olive oil

PREFERRED COOKING METHOD
- Cast iron skillet

Prep Time : 15 min
Total Time : 30 min

INSTRUCTIONS

- In a small bowl, combine chili powder, cumin, paprika, garlic, salt and pepper.
- Season steak with half of the seasoning mixture.
- Add oil to the skillet.
- Add steak to hot skillet, flipping once, until desired doneness, about 4-5 minutes per side for medium rare. Remove and let rest for 5 minutes.
- Season bell peppers and onion with the remaining seasoning mixture
- Add bell peppers and onion to grill, and cook, turning occasionally, until charred and tender, about 6-8 minutes.
- Remove from heat.
- Thinly slice steak against the grain and mix back in with bell peppers and onion.
- Serve with warm tortillas and any additional toppings. Enjoy!

NOTES:

If you somehow have leftovers from this. You can reheat and add some eggs to it in the morning for a delicious high protein breakfast.

GARLIC LIME SHRIMP TACOS

INGREDIENTS

- Corn tortillas
- 2 limes (sliced for serving)
- 1 lb large shrimp (tail off)
- 2 tbsp unsalted butter

TACO SEASONING

- Chili powder
- Paprika
- Onion powder
- Garlic powder
- Cumin
- Dried oregano
- Red pepper flakes
- Salt and pepper

CILANTRO LIME SLAW

- 1/3 cup mayonnaise
- 3 tbsp sour cream
- 1 tsp minced garlic
- 1/4 cup chopped cilantro
- Juice from one lime
- 2 cups finely shredded red/green cabbage

ADDITIONAL TOPPINGS

- Pico de gallo
- Guacamole
- Chopped cilantro

Prep Time : 10 min

Total Time : 20 min

PREFERRED GRILLING METHOD
- Cast iron skillet

INSTRUCTIONS

- Mix the shrimp with the taco seasoning and set aside.
- In a bowl, combine all the ingredients for the cilantro lime sauce. Then pour over the cabbage and mix until well combined. Save some for additional topping.
- In a skillet, melt 2 tbsp butter. Once hot add the shrimp and cook 2 minutes per side, or until pink and opaque. Remove and set aside.
- Warm the tortillas in the skillet and set aside.
- Assemble tacos by adding the cabbage slaw, shrimp, and any desired additional toppings. Drizzle with more cilantro lime sauce and fresh lime juice.
- Serve and enjoy!

CHICKEN LO MEIN

INGREDIENTS

- 8 oz lo mein noodles
- 1 lb boneless skinless chicken breast
- 2 tbsp unsalted butter
- 1 large carrot (julienned)
- 1 red pepper (julienned)
- 3 tbsp minced garlic
- 1 tbsp ginger powder
- Green onions (diced)
- Salt and pepper to taste

SAUCE

- 1/2 cup chicken broth
- 1/4 cup low sodium soy sauce
- 1 tsp sriracha (optional)
- 1 tbsp sesame oil
- 1 tsp cornstarch
- 3 tbsp honey

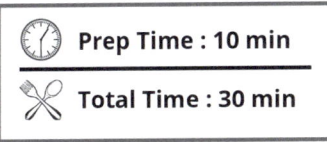

Prep Time : 10 min

Total Time : 30 min

PREFERRED GRILLING METHOD
- Cast iron skillet

INSTRUCTIONS

- Cook noodles according to package instructions. Once cooked, set aside.
- Cut the chicken into strips or cubes.
- Add seseme oil and 1 tbsp of butter to skillet. Once the pan is hot, add the chicken and cook for a couple of minutes before lightly stirring.
- Remove the cooked chicken and set aside.
- Add seseme oil and 1 tbsp of butter to skillet. Add the carrots and bell peppers.
- Saute lightly until the vegetables are cooked. Add in the garlic and ginger and cook until fragrant.
- In a bowl, mix together the sauce ingredients.
- Add the noodles, chicken, and sauce to the skillet. Mix together and bring to a simmer to let the sauce thicken.
- Once the sauce has thickened and the noodles are reheated, garnish with green onions and sesame seeds.
- Serve and enjoy!

CAST IRON CRUSTED PIZZA

INGREDIENTS

- Pizza dough
- 4-6 tbsp olive oil + more if needed
- Shredded mozzarella cheese
- Sliced pepperoni
- Sliced black olives
- Dried oregano
- Pizza sauce

PREFERRED COOKING METHOD
- Cast iron skillet with cover

INSTRUCTIONS

Prep Time : 15 min
Total Time : 30 min

- Preheat the cast iron skillet.
- Add enough olive oil to the bottom of the skillet to completely cover it, about 2-3 tbsp but you may need more or less.
- Using a rolling pin, roll out the dough on a floured surface so it is slightly bigger than the skillet.
- Place dough in the preheated skillet, and cook until it starts to bubble up.
- Use a spatula to check the bottom it should be a light golden color.
- Starting with pizza sauce, add the toppings going all the way to the edges.
- Add cover to skillet and hot coals, and continue to bake until the cheese is completely melted.
- Carefully remove the pizza onto a cutting board to cool.
- Sprinkle oregano on top, slice, serve, and enjoy!

NOTES:

I prefer to have a good pizza dough made ahead of time but you can also use premade canned dough. Most times when I'm making this, I'll have a larger amount of dough ready and cut it into smaller, personal-sized pizzas. Then my kids can add their own toppings themselves and bake separately.

NORTH BEND NACHOS

INGREDIENTS

- Tortilla chips
- Rotisserie chicken (shredded)
- Shredded Mexican cheese blend
- Pico de gallo
- Sliced black olives
- Green onions
- Jalapeños
- Sour cream
- Guacamole

PREFERRED COOKING METHOD
- Cast iron skillet with lid (small batch)
- Dutch oven (larger batches)

Prep Time : 5 min
Total Time : 15 min

INSTRUCTIONS

- Lightly oil the bottom of a large dutch oven, to prevent the nachos from sticking.
- For the first layer, evenly spread tortilla chips into the dutch oven and top with shredded chicken, cheese, and all the other ingredients except for the guacamole and sour cream.
- Repeat for all the other layers. The final size is up to you.
- After the last layer is done, cover the dutch oven and place over your heat source until the cheese has melted.
- Top with sour cream and guacamole.
- Serve and enjoy!

NOTES:

I used to love getting these nachos with a friend at North Bend Bar & Grill. So many great memories and conversations. So make sure when you make these, you have a great group of friends or family around to enjoy them with.

WHITE CHICKEN CHILI

INGREDIENTS

- 2-3 cups shredded chicken
- Monterey jack cheese (shredded)
- 2 cups half & half
- 2 cups chicken broth
- 4 tbsp butter
- 1/4 cup all-purpose flour
- 1 (15 oz) can white corn
- 1 (15 oz) can garbanzo beans
- 1 (15 oz) can white kidney beans
- 1 (15 oz) can great northern beans
- 1 (7 oz) can of diced chilis
- 2 tsp chili powder
- 2 tsp cumin
- Salt and pepper to taste

PREFERRED COOKING METHOD
- Dutch oven

Prep Time : 5 min
Total Time : 20 min

INSTRUCTIONS

- Add butter to dutch oven, then whisk in the flour to create a roux
- Slowly whisk in the chicken broth, then the half & half.
- Whisk in the chili powder, cumin, salt and pepper to taste.
- Add and mix in the shredded chicken.
- Drain all the cans of beans, corn, and diced chilis before adding in.
- Remove from direct heat, cover and simmer for 10-15 minutes.
- Remove from heat, and add shredded cheese and mix until melted.
- Let cool for 5 minutes before serving.
- Serve and top with sour cream and cilantro if desired. Enjoy!

NOTES:

This has been one of my Top 5 favorite things to make for a long time. Especially once we get into Fall and Winter. It's extremely filling, packed with protein and so delicious! This is another recipe I love to make ahead of time and after a long day outside, just reheat it over the fire and you're good to go.

LAKESIDE PAELLA

INGREDIENTS

- 1 lb. large peeled and deveined shrimp
- 8 oz. Spanish chorizo (sliced)
- 1 medium onion (chopped)
- 2 red or yellow bell peppers (1/2" slices)
- 2 tsp saffron threads (finely crushed)
- Salt and pepper to taste
- 3 tbsp minced garlic
- 1 large bay leaf
- 2 cups short-grain rice
- 1 tsp smoked paprika
- 1/2 cup dry white wine
- 4 cups chicken stock
- 2 tsp lemon zest, plus 6 tablespoons juice
- 1 lb. mussels
- 1/2 cup flat-leaf parsley, roughly chopped

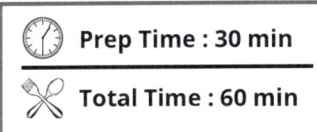

Prep Time : 30 min
Total Time : 60 min

INSTRUCTIONS

- Add shrimp to heated and oiled cast iron skillet and cook for 1-2 minutes, turning once. Transfer to a plate. Remove skillet off of direct heat.
- Add chorizo and cook, stirring constantly, until chorizo begins to crisp and release its oils, 1 to 2 minutes. Transfer half the chorizo to a plate.
- Move back onto direct heat and add onion, bell pepper, saffron, and more oil. Season with salt and pepper. Cook, stirring occasionally, just until tender.
- Add garlic and cook, stirring, until fragrant.
- Add rice and paprika. Cook, stirring, until rice is coated.
- Add wine and cook until almost evaporated. Add chicken stock and 3 tablespoons of lemon juice.
- Bring to a simmer, stirring often, until rice begins to absorb liquid.
- Remove from direct heat, cover, and simmer until most of the liquid is absorbed.
- Add shrimp and mussels to the skillet. Cover and cook until mussels open, shrimp turn pink, and rice is tender.
- Remove from heat and fold in reserved chorizo, and remaining 3 tablespoons lemon juice. Let stand for five minutes. Sprinkle with lemon zest and parsley. Serve with lemon wedges alongside.

SHRIMP FRIED RICE

INGREDIENTS

- 2 pounds medium shrimp (no tail)
- 2 cups frozen peas and diced carrots
- 1 cup canned sweet corn (drained)
- Green onions (chopped)
- 4 tbsp minced garlic
- 4 large eggs lightly beaten
- 4 cups (day old) cooked white rice
- 4 tablespoons low-sodium soy sauce
- 1 tbsp rice wine
- Salt and pepper to taste
- Sesame oil

PREFERRED COOKING METHOD
- Cast iron skillet

Prep Time : 10 min
Total Time : 30 min

INSTRUCTIONS

- Add shrimp to a hot, oiled skillet. Cook for about 5 minutes or until done.
- Remove the shrimp and set aside.
- Add more sesame oil and minced garlic, and cook stirring for 30 seconds.
- Add the peas, carrots, corn, green onions, and cook for about 2 minutes, or until vegetables begin to soften.
- Push vegetables to one side of the skillet, add the lightly beaten eggs to the other side, and cook to scramble, stirring as necessary.
- Add the shrimp back to the skillet.
- Add the rice and evenly drizzle with soy sauce and rice wine, and stir to combine. Cook for about 2 minutes, or until shrimp is heated through.
- Serve warm and enjoy!

NOTES:

> One of the secrets to making great fried rice is using "day old" rice. Don't ask me why, but somehow it makes the difference between good and great!

FIRE ROASTED STUFFED PEPPERS

INGREDIENTS

- Red bell peppers, tops cut off and seeds and insides removed
- 1 lb mild or spicy ground Italian sausage
- 3 cups pre-cooked Spanish-style rice
- 1 ½ cups water
- 1 (15 oz) can fire roasted diced tomatoes
- Shredded Mexican cheese blend
- Green onions for topping

PREFERRED COOKING METHOD
- Dutch oven
- Cast iron skillet

Prep Time : 10 min
Total Time : 35 min

INSTRUCTIONS

- Arrange bell peppers in dutch oven standing up. (If they want to tip over you can cut off the very bottom 1/8" or so to flatten them out and help them stand)
- Cover and cook for 10-15 minutes until tender.
- While peppers are cooking, cook sausage in a skillet, breaking apart with a spatula or spoon as it cooks, until well browned.
- Add rice and tomatoes to the skillet. Stir and cover while peppers finish cooking.
- Mix 1/2 cup cheese into the skillet until melted.
- Spoon the mixture into the baked peppers and top with the remaining cheese.
- Bake for 5 minutes or until cheese is melted.
- Top with green onions if desired. Serve and enjoy!

NOTES:

I like to use the pre-cooked rice with this recipe in order to make things go a little quicker and for easier clean up.

EGGPLANT PARMESAN

INGREDIENTS

- 1 eggplant, sliced into ¼ inch thick slices
- 2 eggs (beaten)
- 1 cup Italian seasoned breadcrumbs
- 1/2 cup grated parmesan cheese
- 1 tbsp garlic powder
- 1 tbsp dried oregano
- Marinara sauce
- Shredded mozzarella cheese
- Fresh basil
- Vegetable oil (for frying)

PREFERRED COOKING METHOD
- Cast iron skillet

Prep Time : 10 min
Total Time : 40 min

INSTRUCTIONS

- In a bowl, combine breadcrumbs, parmesan, garlic powder, and oregano.
- Dip the eggplant slices into the egg, then coat with the breadcrumb mixture, pressing the breadcrumbs onto the eggplant with your hands.
- Heat oil in a cast iron skillet (about ¼ inch deep).
- Fry the breaded eggplant slices in batches for 1-2 minutes per side until golden brown and place on a paper towel-lined plate until all of the slices are fried.
- Discard the oil from the pan. Return the fried eggplant to the skillet and arrange in a circular pattern with the eggplant slices overlapping.
- Top each slice with a tablespoon of marinara sauce (not too much or the eggplant gets soggy) and finish with shredded mozzarella.
- Cover and cook for 25-30 minutes, or until the cheese is bubbly and golden brown.
- Serve with grated parmesan and fresh basil.

NOTES:

You can salt your eggplant slices before frying to remove some of the bitterness from the eggplant. Simply lay the slices out on a paper towel, sprinkle with salt, let sit for 10 minutes or so. Flip and salt the other side, let sit for 10 more minutes, then rinse with water and pat dry.

JAMBALAYA

INGREDIENTS

- 13 oz smoked sausage, cut into ¼" slices
- 1 lb peeled and deveined medium shrimp
- ½ large onion (chopped)
- ½ green bell pepper (chopped)
- ½ red bell pepper (chopped)
- 1 cup chopped celery
- Cajun seasoning
- 2 cups uncooked white rice
- 1 (14.5 ounce) can diced tomatoes
- 2 tbsp minced garlic
- 2 cups chicken broth
- 3 bay leaves
- 1 tsp dried thyme
- Salt and pepper to taste

Prep Time : 20 min
Total Time : 65 min

PREFERRED COOKING METHOD
- Dutch oven

INSTRUCTIONS

- Add and cook the sausage in an oiled and hot dutch oven for 2 minutes.
- Add the onion, bell pepper, and celery. Season with salt, pepper, and cajun seasoning. Cook and stir until the vegetables are soft.
- Stir in the rice until evenly coated in the vegetable mixture, then pour in the tomatoes with juice, garlic, chicken broth, bay leaves, and thyme leaves.
- Bring to a boil, then remove from direct heat, cover and simmer for 20 minutes.
- After 20 minutes, stir in the shrimp, and cook 10 minutes uncovered until the shrimp turn pink and are no longer translucent in the center.
- Remove the pot from the heat, and let stand 5 minutes. Discard the bay leaves.
- Serve hot and enjoy!

NOTES:

Another great recipe for large groups you can make ahead of time and reheat when needed. This helps save time so you can make other sides while this reheats.

GARLIC POTATO STEAK BITES

INGREDIENTS

- 4 tbsp unsalted butter (divided)
- 1 lb. Yukon gold potatoes cut into 1/2" cubes
- 3 garlic cloves, minced
- 1 tsp dried thyme
- 1 tsp dried rosemary
- 1 tsp oregano
- 1 1/2 lbs sirloin steak, cut into 1" cubes
- salt and pepper to taste
- Olive oil

PREFERRED COOKING METHOD
- Cast iron skillet

Prep Time : 5 min
Total Time : 25 min

INSTRUCTIONS

- Heat a large cast iron skillet. Add olive oil and 2 tbsp butter, potatoes, garlic, thyme, rosemary, and oregano. Cook for about 3 minutes, stir, and cook for an additional 5 minutes or until fork tender.
- Remove and set aside into a large bowl.
- Over direct heat. Add the other 2 tbsp butter and steak bites. Let the steak sear on all sides, then continue to stir the steak until they reach 130°F.
- Remove and let rest for a few minutes.
- Mix steak bites into bowl with potatoes.
- Top with fresh herbs, serve, and enjoy!

NOTES:

Another great way to serve this as an appetizer if you have a group is to alternate steak and potato bites on bamboo skewers. Always a favorite!

DESSERTS

WHISKEY CREAM BREAD PUDDING

INGREDIENTS

- 2 cups milk
- 1 ½ cups sugar
- 3 large eggs
- 1 stick butter (melted)
- 1 tbsp vanilla extract
- 1 tbsp cinnamon
- 1 tsp nutmeg
- 10 hamburger buns or other thick bread

WHISKEY CREAM SAUCE

- 1 cup sugar
- 1 stick butter (melted)
- 2 cups heavy cream
- ½ cup Crown Royal (or other whiskey)

PREFERRED COOKING METHOD
- Cast iron skillet or dutch oven
- Cast iron melting pot

Prep Time : 10 min
Total Time : 55 min

INSTRUCTIONS

- Lightly butter cast iron skillet or dutch oven
- In a large bowl, whisk together milk, sugar, and eggs until smooth. Slowly whisk in the melted butter, vanilla, cinnamon, and nutmeg.
- Tear buns or thick bread into 1-inch pieces and add to the wet mixture.
- Lightly mix and mash the buns with a spoon into the wet mixture until moistened. Don't mash them so much that the mixture turns to mush. The bread should be completely moistened with some bun pieces still retaining most of their shape. Add more cinnamon if desired.
- Scrape the mixture into the skillet or dutch oven
- Bake for about 45 minutes, or until the pudding is sponge-like and springs back when touched in the middle. Remove from heat and let rest.
- Combine cream sauce ingredients in a melting pot and bring to a boil for 1 minute. Serve warm over the bread pudding and enjoy!

NOTES:

Remember its bread pudding and not a cake so you don't want it to bake completely through like a cake and dry out.

RICE CRISPY TREAT SMORE'S

INGREDIENTS

- Rice Crispy Treats (homemade or store-bought)
- Mini chocolate chips
- Graham crackers
- Wooden skewers

OPTIONAL TOPPINGS

- Crushed butterfingers
- Reeses peanut butter cups
- Marshmallow cream

PREFERRED COOKING METHOD
- Skewers over hot coals

Prep Time : 2 min
Total Time : 8 min

INSTRUCTIONS

- Pour mini chocolate chips into a bowl.
- Crush graham crackers and put them into another small bowl.
- Press rice crispy treats into the chocolate chips so they stick together.
- Skewer and slowly cook over the hot coals.
- When hot and melty, sprinkle graham crackers over the top.
- Repeat and enjoy!

NOTES:

My kids have made so many delicious variations of these. From using an apple corer and removing the middle of the rice crispy treat to stuff a Reeses peanut butter cup in the middle. To fully dipping it into marshmallow cream and rolling it in a chocolate chip graham cracker mixture. We've wandered down many candy aisles to see what other creative combos we can come up with. Get creative and have fun with this one!

GRILLED HONEY PEACHES

INGREDIENTS

- Fresh peaches (halved and pit removed)
- Brown sugar
- Unsalted butter
- Honey
- Thinly sliced almonds

PREFERRED COOKING METHOD
- Cast iron skillet or griddle

Prep Time : 5 min
Total Time : 15 min

INSTRUCTIONS

- Preheat a skillet or griddle and add butter and brown sugar. Mix together quickly and then add peaches, cut side down.
- Let cook for 3 to 5 minutes while basting the peaches with the melted butter and brown sugar.
- Once cooked to the desired doneness, remove and let slightly cool.
- Top with sliced almonds and honey drizzled over the top.
- Serve and enjoy!

NOTES:

This is a great go to if you don't have the time to make an entire cobbler. It comes together so quickly and if you have the ability, goes perfectly with a scoop of vanilla icecream and fresh granola.

BEBEE BLUEBERRY COBBLER

INGREDIENTS

- 6 cups fresh blueberries (washed & drained)
- 4 tbsp granulated white sugar
- 4 tbsp all-purpose flour
- Juice from one lemon

- 2½ cups all-purpose flour
- 1/2 cup granulated white sugar
- Zest from one lemon
- 2½ tsp baking powder
- ⅔ tsp salt
- 2 large eggs at room temperature
- 1 large egg yolk at room temperature
- 2 cups whole milk at room temperature
- 5 tbsp unsalted butter (melted)

PREFERRED COOKING METHOD
- Cast iron skillet with lid
- Dutch oven

Prep Time : 5 min
Total Time : 80 min

INSTRUCTIONS

- In a large bowl, toss blueberries with 4 tbsp sugar, 4 tbsp flour, and the juice from one large lemon. Set aside.
- In another large bowl, whisk 2½ cups flour, 1/2 cup sugar, lemon zest, baking powder, and salt together.
- Whisk together the eggs, egg yolk, melted butter, and milk.
- Pour the egg mixture into the flour mixture and mix until combined.
- Pour the mixture into a butter-greased skillet or Dutch oven.
- Pour and mix the blueberries into the batter.
- Cover and bake for 65-70 minutes, or until the top is golden brown and the cobbler is cooked through. Make sure to rotate the base and the lid often so it cooks evenly.

NOTES:

I used to live about 10 minutes away from an amazing U-Pick blueberry farm, so we would always have fresh and frozen blueberries on hand throughout the year. This is why this cobbler quickly became a favorite to ensure the blueberries we picked always got used.

CAMPFIRE SHORTCAKES

INGREDIENTS

- 3 cups Bisquick baking mix
- 1 cup milk
- 5 tbsp sugar
- 4 tbsp butter

STRAWBERRY MIXTURE

- 4 cups sliced strawberries
- 3 tbsp sugar
- 1 tbsp lemon juice
- Whipped cream for topping

PREFERRED COOKING METHOD
- Cast iron skillet with lid
- Dutch oven

Prep Time : 10 min
Total Time : 30 min

INSTRUCTIONS

- In a medium side bowl add 3 cups Original Bisquick baking mix, 1 cup milk, 4 tbsp melted butter, and 5 tbsp sugar. Mix until combined, then set aside.
- Drop your dough by large spoonfuls into grease skillet or dutch oven.
- Sprinkle a pinch of sugar over each biscuit.
- Cover and cook for 10 minutes. Check for doneness and add additional time as needed until fully cooked.
- As biscuits cook, prep the strawberries. Slice 3-4 cups of fresh strawberries and place in a bowl. Mix in 3 tbsp. sugar and 1 tbsp lemon juice.
- Biscuits will be done when soft on the inside and a light golden color on top.
- Remove cooked biscuits and set aside.
- Top each biscuit with a generous helping of whipped topping and strawberries.
- Serve and enjoy!

LANDON'S NUTELLA CREPES

INGREDIENTS

- ½ cup lukewarm water
- 1 cup milk, warm
- 4 large eggs
- 2 tbsp vanilla extract
- 4 tbsp unsalted butter (melted)
- 1 cup all-purpose flour
- 2 tbsp granulated sugar
- Pinch of sea salt

OPTIONAL FILLINGS

- Whipped cream
- Fresh berries
- Nutella
- Peanut butter and banana slices
- Canned apple filling and cinnamon

PREFERRED COOKING METHOD
- Cast iron skillet or griddle

Prep Time : 5 min
Total Time : 15 min

INSTRUCTIONS

- Add and whisk the ingredients in the order they are listed, starting with the wet ingredients. Once well combined, set aside so the bubbles can go down.
- Melt a dot of butter in a skillet.
- Pour about 1/4 cup batter into a preheated skillet and swirl the skillet around so the batter thinly and evenly coats the bottom.
- Once the edges are almost golden, flip the crepe using a thin-edged spatula to easily get under the crepe.
- Cook another 20 seconds or until the second side turns golden then turn the crepe out onto a clean cutting board.
- Repeat with the remaining batter, adding butter as needed.
- Fill crepes with your choice of fillings and roll. Top with any additional fillings.
- Serve and enjoy!

NOTES:

Although these are easy to satisfy your sweet tooth. I also love to make these crepes with more hearty and filling options. Some of my favorites lately have been eggs/ham/swiss cheese, and smoked salmon with herb cream cheese.

CONNOR'S ELEPHANT EARS

INGREDIENTS

- Flour tortillas
- Granulated sugar
- Cinnamon
- Canola oil (enough to fill the bottom of a small pot)
- Whipped cream
- Bamboo skewers

PREFERRED COOKING METHOD
- Cast iron pot
- Small Dutch oven

Prep Time : 5 min
Total Time : 15 min

INSTRUCTIONS

- In a large bowl, mix together cinnamon and sugar. The amount will depend on how many you are making and how much cinnamon you prefer.
- Add oil to your pot and using a candy thermometer bring temperature to 375°F
- While your oil is heating, loosely roll your flour tortillas into a cone shape.
- The trick to this is using a bamboo skewer to keep the tortilla in its cone shape. Do so by starting at the top and piercing the tortilla in and out towards the bottom where the edges all come together.
- Once the oil reaches 375°F, dip the tortillas into the oil making sure it fills the inside. After a few dunks, the tortilla will be puffy and golden brown.
- Then transfer to the large bowl of cinnamon and sugar. Roll and sprinkle the inside as well. Then shake off the excess. Set aside, and repeat with the rest of the tortillas.
- Once done, fill with whipped cream and serve immediately. ENJOY!

NOTES:

By far one of our favorites if you don't mind the cleanup. We also love topping the whipped cream with strawberry or chocolate sauce!

RECOMMENDATIONS

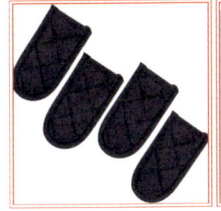

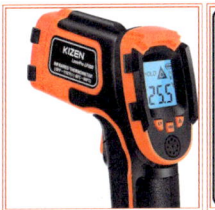

INDEX

PREFACE..2

APPETIZERS
Grilled Shrimp Skewers..5
Chicken Quesadilla...6
Flatbread Margherita Pizza..7
Grilled Stuffed Mushrooms..8
Buffalo Cauliflower Bites..9
Prosciutto Wrapped Asparagus..10
Stuff Jalapeños...11

SIDES
Smoked Bacon Mac & Cheese...13
Watermelon Feta Salad..14
Grilled Street Elotes..15
Stuffed Romaine Hearts..16
Chicken Quinoa Salad..17
French Bread Pizza..18

BREAKFAST
Watershed Breakfast Burritos...20
Smoked Biscuits & Gravy...21
Stuffed French Toast..22
Bacon Pancakes..23
Sausage & Potato Hash..24
Early Bird Donut Holes..25
Sunrise Casserole..26
Chelan Style Calzones...27
Fire Crusted Quiche...28
Honey Butter Cornbread...29

INDEX

ENTREES

Beef Stew..31
Back Country Lasagna..32
Chicken and Potato Chowder..33
Dutch Oven Enchiladas...34
Steak Fajitas..35
Garlic Lime Shimp Tacos..36
Chicken Lo Mein..37
Cast Iron Crusted Pizza..38
North Bend Nachos..39
White Chicken Chili..40
Lakeside Paella..41
Shrimp Fried Rice..42
Fire Roasted Stuffed Peppers...43
Eggplant Parmesan..44
Jambalaya...45
Garlic Potato Steak Bites...46

DESSERTS

Whiskey Cream Bread Pudding..48
Rice Crispy Treat Smore's..49
Grilled Honey Peaches...50
Bebee Blueberry Cobbler...51
Campfire Shortcakes..52
Landon's Nutella Crepes..53
Connor's Elephant Ears...54

RECOMMENDATIONS...55

"In every walk with nature,
one receives far more than he seeks"
— John Muir